Logan's Run

William F. Nolan and George Clayton Johnson

Level 3

Retold by Kathy Burke

Series Editors: Andy Hopkins and Jocelyn Potter

Pearson Education Limited
Edinburgh Gate, Harlow,
Essex CM20 2JE, England
and Associated Companies throughout the world.

ISBN: 978-1-4082-3202-6

This edition first published by Pearson Education Ltd 2010

3 5 7 9 10 8 6 4

Text copyright © Pearson Education Ltd 2010

Illustrations by Raul Allen

The moral rights of the authors have been asserted in accordance
with the Copyright Designs and Patents Act 1988

Set in 11/13pt A. Garamond
Printed in China
SWTC/03

Published by Pearson Education Ltd in association with Penguin Books Ltd,
both companies being subsidiaries of Pearson Plc

Acknowledgements
We are grateful to the following for permission to reproduce photographs:

(Key: b-bottom; c-centre; l-left; r-right; t-top)

Alamy Images: Borderlands 72tr; Iain Masterton 72tl; Tom Uhlman 72bl;
Getty Images: David Silverman 72br; **iStockphoto:** 74br; Jeremy Edwards 74tr;
Alexander Hafemann 74bl; **Jupiter Unlimited:** Goodshoot 74tl2

All other images © Pearson Education

Picture Research by: by Hilary Luckcock

Every effort has been made to trace the copyright holders and we apologise in advance
for any unintentional omissions. We would be pleased to insert the appropriate
acknowledgement in any subsequent edition of this publication.

For a complete list of the titles available in the Penguin Active Reading series please
write to your local Pearson Longman office or to: Penguin Readers Marketing Department,
Pearson Education, Edinburgh Gate, Harlow, Essex CM20 2JE, England.

Contents

1.1 What's the book about?

1 Look at the picture on the front cover of the book. Then read the information about the story on the back cover. Is this book (✓):

a ☐ a detective story?

b ☐ a love story?

c ☐ a science fiction story?

2 These words are important in the story. Check their meanings at the bottom of the pages in Chapters 1 and 2. Then match the words to the sentences.

chase	hell	maze	muscle	net
	palm	sanctuary	violence	

a You can lose your way in this. ....

b Dogs often do this to cats. ....

c You can catch fish in this. ....

d These are parts of your body. ....

e This is a part of your body. ....

f This isn't a good place. ....

g Guns or knives are often used for this. ....

1.2 What happens first?

1 Read the chapter titles, and the words in *italics* on pages 2 and 4. Then look at the pictures on pages 3 and 11. What do you think? Discuss these questions.

a Why is the girl afraid?

b Who is the dead man? Who killed him and why?

c What is Last Day?

2 There are some words in the story, in *italics*, that you won't find in a dictionary. Look at these examples. Guess the meanings of the words.

a Logan shot a *nitro* into the group and killed three of them.

b A police *paravane* landed silently near the man.

c He walked to the *communideck*, put the key in, and turned it. The screen lit up ...

*T*he problems started one hot summer in the 1960s. Angry young people around the world wanted older people and governments to know how they felt. In Washington D.C., and in other cities, there was **violence** in the streets and in colleges.

Young Americans wanted change.

By the 1970s, 75% of the people on Earth were less than twenty-one years old.

The number of young people continued to grow.

In the 1980s, they were 79.7% of the population.

In the 1990s, 82.4%.

In the year 2000, almost 100%.

violence /ˈvaɪələns/ (n) attacks on people who you want to hurt or kill

CHAPTER 1

The Chase

In the moonlight she saw the face of a Sandman—his cold eyes, his hard mouth. His finger moved and she heard the gun explode.

The girl's eyes were wild with fear. They shone out of her dirty face. Her knees were covered in blood from the fall. She had a sharp pain in her side from running. But she ran.

There was a high lovers' moon and the night was full of dark shadows. The shadows followed her. The shadows could kill her.

When did she cross the river? Was it last night or the night before? Where was she now? She didn't know. To her right she could see a high wall. A **Nursery**. Maybe her baby was there! She moved to the left, into the night-black between buildings. She came to another wall. She turned around. Should she go back across the river again? She had to continue but she wanted to rest. She *needed* to rest.

Wait! She heard a noise. Someone was there in the shadows.

It was a Sandman*!

A silent scream went through her.

She tried to climb the wall. She tried to lift her tired body up. "Please! Please!" But she couldn't do it. The wall was too high. She fell onto the ground, crying.

She sat there and looked at the **palm** of her right hand. A black flower shone there. A few days ago, the light from the flower was a warm blood-red; seven years before that, it was sky-blue, and seven years before that it was sun-yellow. A different color for each seven years of her life. Now she was twenty-one and the flower was black. Sleep black. Death black.

The man moved toward her in the dark. She looked at her palm, because her future and her past were written there. All of her fears and hopes were there. In the past, **Sanctuary** was her hope—her dream. She didn't want to die like the others. She didn't want Sleep. She wanted to live. But that was impossible. There was no hope now.

The man stood over her. She didn't look up. She knew that it was the end. And so she dreamed. She was not there—a criminal, hated and **terrified**. She

---

* Sandman: a man in children's stories who brings sleep and happy dreams. In this story, *Sandmen* bring death.

nursery /ˈnɜːsəri/ (n) a place where young children are looked after by adults
palm /pɑːm/ (n) the inside part of your hand
sanctuary /ˈsæŋktʃuˌeri/ (n) a safe place that protects people from danger
terrified /ˈterəˌfaɪd/ (adj) very afraid

was in Sanctuary. It was a warm summer's afternoon. She was lying in the long grass, looking up at the clear blue sky. She wasn't thinking about time. There was no time in this world. No worry.

So why did her hand move to the knife under her clothes? Why did she want to push that knife into her heart? Why?

The man pointed a gun at her.

The *homer*!

In the moonlight she saw the face of the Sandman—his cold eyes, his hard mouth. His finger moved and she heard the gun **explode**. That was the last sound that she heard. Then there was only pain—terrible, unimaginable pain.

It was *the end*.

explode /ɪkˈspləʊd/ (v) to make a sudden, loud noise before something breaks into pieces. A gas *explosion* can destroy a house.

CHAPTER 2

Last Day

Doyle threw the terrified girl forward and ran. The tangler
net went around the screaming girl and held her tightly.

Logan was tired but the little man didn't stop talking.
"You know what it's like," he said. "Nobody does everything that they want to do in their life. All the traveling, all the girls ... I'm the same. I'd like to live to twenty-five, thirty ... but it isn't going to happen. I can accept that. I've lived a good life. I've had good times. I'm not afraid. After I'm gone, nobody will say that Sawyer was afraid!"

He talked and talked. Logan knew why. If he talked, he didn't have to think. Logan saw this all the time. Everyone talked a lot on Last Day.

Sawyer looked at his palm. The flower was red, then black, then red again. Logan could see the worry in his eyes.

"Do you believe the Thinker ever makes mistakes?" Sawyer asked Logan. "It doesn't feel like I'm twenty-one. It really doesn't. I remember the day when I became fourteen. How long ago was it when my flower changed? I'm sure it wasn't more than five years ago."

Logan wasn't listening. He was thinking about his fourteenth birthday.

"No," said Sawyer, not waiting for Logan to answer. "I'm sure that the Thinker doesn't make mistakes."

He was silent for a minute. Then, in a quiet voice, he said, "I guess I'm afraid."

"Most people are," said Logan.

"Well, maybe I *am* afraid but I'm not going to run. No! The Thinker is right. We have to keep the number of people down. I won't run!"

The two men sat quietly while the car traveled through the **Maze**.

Finally, Sawyer spoke again.

"Do you think the *homer* is really so terrible?"

"Yes," said Logan. "I believe it is."

"People say that it feels your body heat. That's how it finds you. Then it burns you! It completely destroys your body—in seconds!"

Logan didn't speak.

Sawyer's face was gray. A **muscle** moved near his mouth.

"God," he said, looking down at the floor.

---

maze /meɪz/ (n) a place with many paths that is very difficult to find your way through. In this story, people travel under ground through the *Maze*.
muscle /ˈmʌsəl/ (n) a part of the body that helps you move. *Muscles* become bigger and stronger with exercise. In this story, Muscle is also the name of a drug.

Then the color returned to his face.

"Of course, it's necessary. Runners have to be punished. They don't *have* to run, do they? A Sleepshop isn't so bad, is it? I saw one when I was twelve. In Paris. It was clean and nice."

Logan thought of the Sleepshops with their brightly painted rooms and restful music. The assistants wore warm colors and spoke softly. And then, of course, there was the drug, *Hallucinogen*. When people took this, their worries left them. Their faces showed only happiness. They moved slowly, as in a dream. Logan thought of the dark rooms downstairs with metal shelves. On those shelves were hundreds of boxes with the names and numbers of men and women on them.

"No," he said. "They're not bad."

Sawyer was talking again. "But I could never do what those Sandmen have to do. I'm not saying that runners are right! They're criminals! But how can a Sandman use a *homer* on a man? How can he do that?"

"I get off here," said Logan.

He left the car.

Logan didn't live in this area. He had a long walk now but Sawyer was making him angry. He knew this part of the city. He remembered killing a man here. He put the memory out of his mind and continued walking, through the crowds of people. People in a hurry, with empty eyes, going nowhere. A young man was sitting on the ground with a sign around his neck. The sign said *RUN*! He was trying to give out pieces of paper but people only shouted at him.

"Dirty Runner!" "Trash!" "You're sick!"

The man sat and smiled.

Logan took one of the papers and read it:

DO NOT ACCEPT SLEEP! RUN!

MEN SHOULD LIVE THEIR FULL LIVES!

DON'T ACCEPT DEATH AT TWENTY-ONE!

A police *paravane* landed silently near the man. Logan watched two policemen in yellow coats walk toward him. He didn't run. The police took him away and the *paravane* lifted into the evening sky.

A woman was standing next to Logan.

"Thank God for the police," she said. "Those people are crazy! It's terrifying!"

The sky was dark now and the evening stars were shining. Logan stopped to watch that evening's Maze News report. A man's face lit up a **huge screen** on the front of the Maze News building.

huge /hyudʒ/ (adj) very, very large
screen /skriːn/ (n) the flat, glass part on the front of a TV or computer

"Good evening," he said to the crowds. "Fourteen people were killed today during a Gypsy* gang war in Stafford Heights. Police caught four of the Gypsies and are looking for the others. They *will* find them." The man looked very serious, and was silent for a minute. Then he continued.

"The runner Harry 7 was caught by police earlier today in the Trancas area. He was sent to **Hell**. His friends were invited to say goodbye but nobody came. What does that show us? It shows us that we are good people, law-loving people. There is no place for runners in our world! And we must …"

Logan stopped listening and moved away. A girl walked toward him.

"You aren't happy," she said, putting her hand on his arm.

He moved away from her and continued walking.

"I can make you happy!" she called after him.

Happy. Logan thought about the word. She was right, of course. He *was* unhappy. Words came into his mind: *You can't buy happiness.* But, of course, in this world you could.

He turned down a side street and started walking toward Roeburt. The drug palace in Roeburt was the city's largest, with the best drugs. The friendly, white-coated assistants knew how to give you a great time. They helped you forget.

"LF please," Logan said.

"How much would you like?" asked the assistant, a young man.

"The usual," he answered.

The man took him to a Blueroom. It was empty except for a large armchair

---

* Gypsy: one of a group of people who travel around and live in many different places

Hell /hɛl/ (n) the place where, it is believed in some religions, bad people are punished

and a small table. Logan sat in the chair and took the drug.

"Have a good lift," the man said as he left.

Logan closed his eyes for a minute so the drug could work. When he opened them, the room was filled with a terrible light. It was a bad lift.

He was falling, falling from a window.

A man caught him.

"You were running. That's OK," said the man.

"No. I wasn't! I wasn't running! I fell! I fell from a window," Logan shouted.

Suddenly there was fire all around him. He ran through the fire. Voices were everywhere, calling "Black flower! Black flower!".

Where was his gun? He needed his gun. The man caught him again.

"Running again?" he smiled. But now Logan had the gun. Nothing could hurt him. The homer hit the man and the world exploded.

When he left the Blueroom, the assistant smiled at him.

"You were really lifted. Would you like another one?"

"No, thanks."

Logan didn't feel better. He left the drug palace and walked toward the colored lights on the Glasshouse. The words shone out at him.

HAPPINESS!
DREAM GIRLS!

"Your happiness makes us happy, sir," an assistant said, unsmiling.

Logan could see the bodies moving inside each room. The floors and walls were made of glass. Different rooms lit up at different times to show the enjoyment of the men and women inside them.

Logan took a girl into one of the rooms.

"Lie down," she said, and came onto the glass bed with him.

He felt the eyes all around them, watching them. Hours passed.

When morning came, Logan got up silently. He left the girl and went back home, to his room. It was time for work. No time to sleep. His muscles hurt. His eyes were red. He took a shower but it didn't help.

He got dressed, put on his long, black Sandman coat, and left for work.

Francis was waiting for him when he arrived. He smiled at Logan.

"You look terrible," he said. "Bad night?"

Francis never looked bad. No lifts or Glasshouses for him. Never before a job. Francis was clear-headed and calm. Why couldn't Logan be like that? Very few Sandmen had Francis's skill and intelligence. He wasn't like other men. He had no real friends. No one knew about any lovers. He had a long, thin body and the black eyes of a wild cat. He was a smooth, silent killer. *And what does he think of me?* Logan often asked himself. *He's always smiling and friendly but judging every move.*

They walked toward the Gun Room together. Logan was nervous. His hands were wet. He needed his gun. He was always fine with a gun in his hand, **chasing** a runner somewhere in the city. He felt good when he was doing his job.

The two men came to a high metal door.

"Names?" asked a computerized voice.

Each man put the palm of his hand on the door. It opened and they went into the Gun Room. Only a Sandman could carry a gun and no other person could use it. It was too dangerous. Logan checked that his gun was ready: *tangler, ripper, needler, nitro, vapor*—and *homer*. All good. He held the gun and felt strong again.

Francis and Logan then walked to the Report Room. A nervous-looking assistant hurried toward them.

"We've had a lot of problems today. I can't find Webster 16 and we've got a runner in Pavilion, moving east."

"Who's going to take him?" asked Logan.

"You are," said the assistant. "Francis will help if you need him."

"All right," said Logan. "Give me the information."

"Name: Doyle 10-14302. His flower blacked at five thirty-nine. That's eighteen minutes ago. He's moving east but he's not going near the Maze. I think he knows about the cameras there. He's moving toward Arcade. Be careful. He's probably dangerous."

Logan pressed the numbers 10-14302 into a computer and the information on Doyle came up on the screen: photo, height, age, names of friends. Logan read Doyle's flower history: YELLOW: 0-7 years. Parented by a machine in a Missouri Nursery. BLUE: 7-14. The usual. Lived in lots of different states, traveled around Europe. No criminal activities. RED: 14-21. Difficult. Problems with police. Attacked a Sandman. Three girlfriends. One of them tried to help runners. A sister, Jessica 6: no problems with police.

Logan studied Doyle's photo. He was a big man, as tall as Logan, dark hair, a strong face. An easy face to remember. Easy to find in a crowd. He took the small black *follower* from his belt and pressed in Doyle's numbers. Then he returned to Francis.

Francis was standing in front of a large screen, watching a moving red light—Doyle.

"He's not our usual kind of runner," said Francis. "I've watched him. He knows exactly where he's going. He has information and he's not making any mistakes. Call me if you need help."

The **chase** began. Logan got off the walkway at the main station and saw Doyle getting out of a car. Doyle saw Logan's black coat and ran into the crowds. He was still moving east—toward Arcade. Logan tried to follow him but Doyle caught another car. *Good,* thought Logan. *He'll run. He'll get tired.*

He watched him on the *follower.* The assistant was right. Doyle knew about the cameras in the Maze. He was staying above ground and still trying to get to Arcade. Logan showed himself in the crowds. He wanted Doyle to see his black coat. He wanted to scare him. But Doyle knew what he was doing. He continued moving. He stayed in the crowds.

The guy's smart, thought Logan. He watched Doyle on his *follower.* He was very near—coming down in an elevator. Logan moved fast. As the elevator doors opened, Logan lifted his gun. Doyle started to get out and saw him. His face turned white. He couldn't escape the *homer.*

Logan prepared to shoot and … stopped. Why?

In that second Doyle escaped back into the elevator. Down … down …

Logan shouted. What happened? Why didn't he shoot Doyle? He watched the red light move south on his *follower,* then followed the elevator down.

When the doors opened, Doyle was holding a young girl in front of him.

Logan shot the *tangler* at Doyle. Doyle threw the terrified girl forward and ran. The *tangler* **net** went around the screaming girl and held her tightly. Logan called a police *paravane* to help her. He then continued after Doyle.

There he was. In the crowds again. The *homer* couldn't find Doyle in all these people. In a crowd, he had to walk to a runner, press the gun into his stomach, and shoot. But Doyle was too fast.

The chase continued. Doyle was moving east again, still trying for Arcade. Logan moved quickly but Doyle was traveling west now, into Cathedral. This was bad. Logan could lose Doyle there. He called Francis.

"He tricked me," he told Francis. "He's not going to Arcade. It's Cathedral! We have to stop him before he gets there! Meet me at the bridge."

chase /tʃeɪs/ (n/v) the act of following someone quickly. You *chase* them because you want to catch them.
net /nɛt/ (n) material with many holes in it, used to catch things like fish

Cathedral: a dark, ugly part of Los Angeles, full of burned buildings—a place of danger, violence, and sudden death. The home of the Cub Scouts*. Logan knew about Cathedral's bloody history. Runners never came out again. The Cubs killed them. When police officers went in there they, too, were never seen again.

Logan found Francis at the bridge. He was hurt.

"Doyle hit me from behind," he said. "This guy's dangerous."

Logan looked at his *follower* again. Doyle was very near. Logan looked around and finally saw him. He was running across the bridge. But he kept his head low, protected by the stone side wall.

Suddenly, on the other side, there were more shadows moving in the darkness. *Cubs!* Logan watched them walk toward Doyle. There was something strange about their movements.

"They've taken Muscle," said Francis.

"Where do they get it?" asked Logan.

Before the Little War, soldiers took it to make them strong and fast. But they became too violent, so the government stopped the use of the drug.

Logan and Francis watched the Cubs move in and attack Doyle. He fell to the ground. The Cubs hit him and kicked him again and again.

"We'll try gas," said Francis.

They shot the Cubs with *vapors*. The gas drove the Cubs away from Doyle immediately. He lay on the ground, not moving.

"I'll go and check him. You watch for the Cubs," said Francis.

But Francis didn't get far. The Cubs came back and started attacking him. Logan shot a *nitro* into the group and killed three of them. He ran to Doyle. The man's face was a bloody mess. He was trying to speak.

"Sanctuary," he said. Then his head fell back. He was dead.

His hand opened and something fell out. It was a key. Logan quickly put it in his pocket.

"Dead?" Francis asked.

"Yes," Logan answered.

Francis looked down at the bloody body.

"He was *ours*. Not *theirs*," he said angrily. He took out his gun and shot a *blister* into Doyle's body. The body exploded and disappeared.

"Let's go," said Francis.

They traveled back to the Report Room in silence. Logan kept his right hand closed. He didn't want Francis to see the flower in his palm.

It was starting to change color …

* Cub Scouts: in our world, boys who belong to a special club. At meetings, they learn new skills. In this story, Cub Scouts are very dangerous boys.

2.1 Were you right?

Look back at Activity 1.2.1 on page iv. Then read the sentences below. Are they right (✓) or wrong (✗)?

1 ☐ The girl is killed by a Sandman.

2 ☐ Doyle is killed by a Sandman.

3 ☐ A runner is a person who is trying to escape death.

4 ☐ People take the drug Muscle to look good.

5 ☐ Logan is a Sandman.

6 ☐ Logan enjoys his life.

7 ☐ Logan and Francis are good friends.

8 ☐ Logan tells Francis about the key.

2.2 What more did you learn?

Match the words below with a picture. Write the letters A–F.

1 ☐ Last Day

2 ☐ a Sleepshop

3 ☐ *tangler, ripper, needler, nitro, vapor,* and *homer*

4 ☐ a Sandman

5 ☐ the police

6 ☐ a *communideck*

2.3 Language in use

Look at the sentences on the right. Then use the verbs below and complete the story with the correct past progressive forms.

> She **was lying** in the long grass, **looking up** at the clear blue sky.
>
> She **wasn't thinking** about time.

| fly | hurry | look | go | shout | laugh | smile | throw |

It was evening. The sun ¹.................................... down behind the tall buildings. Police *paravanes* ².................................... in the dark sky. The streets were full of people. They ³.................................... along the streets. They ⁴.................................... at the ground. Nobody ⁵..................................... A man ⁶.................................... at the crowds, "Don't accept death! Run! Live!" Some people ⁷.................................... things at him. A little boy ⁸.................................... at him.

2.4 What happens next?

Read the title of Chapter 3 and the words in *italics* below it. Then look at the pictures in Chapter 3. Discuss these questions and write notes.

1 What does Logan decide to do? Why?

....

....

2 Who does he meet in this chapter?

....

....

3 Where does he go?

....

....

4 What has happened to him by the end of the chapter?

....

....

Logan's Run

"Your brother's dead but we're alive. And if we want to stay alive,
we'll have to keep moving."

L ogan got back to his room late, showered, and changed. He pressed "meal search," and dinner and a drink arrived. He sat with his drink and looked at his palm. It was changing from red to black, black to red … Last Day. Twenty-four hours to live.

He picked up the key. Doyle's key. Did this key take a man to Sanctuary? Was there really a Sanctuary, a place where runners could escape death? *If this is true*, thought Logan, *I must try to find it. I must destroy it. Then I can be proud of my life.*

He walked to the *communideck*, put the key in, and turned it. The screen lit up and a girl's face looked at Logan. She was about sixteen, with dead eyes.

"Call back later," she said. "I'm going out."

"I'm calling now," answered Logan.

"Have you got a name?"

"Yes."

"Are you going to give it to me?" Her eyes began to show some interest.

"Sanctuary," Logan said the word.

"Who gave you my key?" she asked.

"A friend."

"I'm going out."

"You said that."

"To a party."

"I can meet you there," said Logan.

She studied him for a minute.

"Halstead, West End. Apartment 2582. I really shouldn't invite strangers. If you aren't strong enough, I'll be in trouble."

"I'm strong enough," Logan answered.

She said one last thing before the screen went black. "I'm Lilith. I think you'll find me … helpful.

The party in 2582 was crazy when Logan arrived. A man in an orange suit answered the door. He was drunk.

"Come in! Enjoy!"

Logan walked past him and looked around the crowded, smoke-filled room. No Lilith.

"Here. Have one of these." A tall dark-haired girl was standing in front of him, holding a large glass with something pink in it."

"No, thanks."

'You men are all the same. Afraid of anything new."

"Maybe you need a *boy*," Logan said.

"Very funny. I'm fifteen. I'm a woman and I need a man. How old are you?"

"Old enough," answered Logan. He kept his right hand closed. He could feel the heat of the flower in his palm.

"You're unhappy," she said. "I like that. Do you want to spend some time together?"

"No. No, thanks."

Her voice went cold. "Loser."

She turned and walked away.

Where was Lilith? The door opened and a fat man with a big smile came in. His arms were full of brightly colored clothes.

"The stuff's here! Time for fun, everybody!" he shouted.

"Did you think I wasn't coming?" Suddenly Lilith was standing in front of Logan, dressed in a tight silver dress and high boots.

"Let's talk," said Logan. "You know why I'm here."

The fat man ran toward them and pushed purple bodysuits into their arms.

"Get dressed and let's spy!" he shouted.

"We'll work together," said Lilith.

Logan went into the changing room and took off his clothes. His gun was a problem. He couldn't wear it under the skintight bodysuit. He hid it at the back of the closet.

When he came out, Lilith was waiting for him with a large drink.

"Thanks. I need this," Logan said, and drank it quickly.

The fat man gave everyone cameras.

"Happy spying!" he shouted.

Lilith and Logan climbed higher and higher inside the building. They looked down into the Glasshouses, filming the people in them. Logan had to be careful. Spying was illegal and he didn't want the police to stop him. The police never questioned a Sandman but he couldn't show the police his gun. He didn't want Lilith to know that he was a Sandman.

"Here, hold my feet. I'm going down," she said.

Logan held her feet. Lilith hung upside down outside a window, filming the lovers inside. She was a long way above the ground. Below her was only black emptiness. Did she really know anything about Sanctuary or did she just love danger?

When she finished filming, he pulled her up.

"Can't we talk now?" he asked.

"You're doing well," she laughed, and started climbing again.
Logan followed until they got to the roof.
"Jump!" Lilith shouted.
She jumped off the roof and down onto another building. Logan followed her.

"Here's a good one!" she said. "You film this time."

Logan filmed the people inside.

"Great!" said Lilith.

"Now we talk!" said Logan.

"OK. What do you know about Sanctuary?" she asked.

"I know that I want to go there."

"Where did you get my key?" She watched him carefully.

"I ... I ..." Logan's mouth felt strange. He couldn't stop smiling. "From the same place that all runners get theirs." He started laughing and couldn't stop. *What was happening to him?* He lifted off the ground. He was in Space ... flying in Space ...

"Answer the question." Lilith was close, speaking quietly into his ear.

Logan was singing a children's song. He was in Space, looking down at himself. He watched Lilith hit his face and pull his head back.

"The key! Where did you get the key?"

Logan's neck hurt. He stood up. Lilith was holding onto him. The world was suddenly filled with orange light that hurt his eyes.

"Did you kill Doyle?" Lilith was still there, shouting now.

The orange light was warm. He wanted to sleep ...

"Doyle 10. Cubs ... Cubs killed him," he said quietly.

He was lying on the roof of the building now. His body ached. Then he realized. A **truth** drug—in his drink!

"What now?" he asked her.

"Now you see Doc," she said.

"Doc who?" he asked.

"You'll find him in Arcade. Look for *The New You*. That's his place. That was a great lift, eh?" She was smiling.

"Yes, a great lift."

A short time later, Logan left the walkway at Beverly station and moved through the crowds in Arcade.

Arcade was a crazy place, always busy, always filled with people. You could find everything there: sex, drugs, Re-Live stores. Strange sounds and smells were everywhere.

Logan walked slowly, looking for Doc's. Then he saw the sign.

THE NEW YOU!
FAST SERVICE!
LOW PRICES!
GREAT RESULTS!

truth /truθ/ (n) the true facts or information about something

Logan went into the store. The waiting room was empty. A bored-looking girl was sitting behind a desk.

"You want Doc?" she asked, in a tired voice.

"I want Sanctuary," answered Logan.

The girl took his hand, turned it over, and looked at his palm.

"Follow me," she said, sounding bored, "Follow me for the new you."

She took him to a large white room. In the middle of the room was a metal bed. Hanging above the bed was a huge machine. *Table!*

"There's not a better one between here and Alaska," said a hard voice.

Logan turned and saw a sixteen-year-old boy in a long white doctor's coat. So this was Doc.

"You're a little nervous, aren't you?" Doc laughed. "That's OK. Runners are nervous people. You've come to me early. That's smart. Usually people wait until the Sandman's chasing them. It's so difficult to do good work then. So, what do you want? New face? Body too? What do you think?"

"Just the face," Logan answered.

"Not much time, eh? Runners never have time. I won't ask your name. Don't want to know. You've got the key. That's good enough for me. Ballard knows who to give the keys to."

Ballard! The world's oldest man. The man who—the stories said—started Sanctuary.

"Holly will get you ready," Doc said. "Don't worry about the Table. They call me Doc but I'm good with machines too—all kinds of machines. I can make anything out of anything. Believe me!"

While Doc was talking, Holly started to take Logan's shirt off. His gun was inside his shirt.

"Do I have to take my clothes off?" he asked.

"No," the girl answered. "But empty your pockets."

She then took him to the metal bed. The heavy machine hung above it, with its knives, lights, and switches. Logan was terrified but he got on. Holly tied his hands and feet to the bed.

"Ask him to give you dark hair," she said quietly into his ear. "I like it."

"Anything special?" asked Doc. "I can give you almost anything."

"You decide. Just *do* it," Logan answered angrily.

"Keep calm." Doc said. "You runners are always in a hurry. Always pushing me. But you won't go anywhere without Doc. Understand? You can't use the key until 9:30. We have time. Plenty of time for the new you!"

He started pulling switches and the machine began to move down, nearer to Logan. An **alarm** suddenly sounded and the machine stopped.

"Did you empty your pockets?"

"He did," Holly answered.

"Well, *something's* wrong," said Doc.

Before Logan could speak, Doc pulled open his shirt.

"A gun! We have a Sandman! Lock the door, Holly!" he shouted.

"You've seen my hand!" said Logan. "I'm on Last Day. How can I be a Sandman if I'm running?"

"You have a gun," said Doc. "Only Sandmen have guns."

"OK, but I'm not the first Sandman to run!" shouted Logan.

"Why should I believe you?" answered Doc. "You're going to get more than a new face!"

He pulled a large red switch and the Table came to life. Sharp knives lowered from the machine. Logan tried to free his hands but he couldn't. One

alarm /əˈlɑrm/ (n) a loud noise that tells people about danger

of the knives caught his knee. Another cut his right shoulder. Down it came again, cutting the tie around Logan's right hand.

Logan reached for his gun, and Doc and the girl ran out of the room. Logan quickly freed his other hand and his feet and jumped off the Table. The machine was now attacking the metal bed, metal against metal, screaming.

Logan tried to plan his next move. He needed a second key from Doc to continue his run. He had to get him. He kicked open the door and ran through the dark building.

Something flew out of the shadows and hit his arm. He dropped his gun. His arm felt like ice. A *popsickle*! Doc was coming toward him now, holding the shining police ice stick. One hit on your chest froze your body in seconds. Death.

Logan waited. When he could see Doc clearly, he kicked him in the stomach. Doc fell to his knees, screaming. Logan gave another strong kick to Doc's head. The boy fell silently to the ground.

Logan quickly searched the boy's pockets. No key. Then he heard a noise from the next room. He moved carefully to the door and opened it slowly. Holly was standing against the wall, holding a knife to her heart. She was terrified. Logan lifted his gun to shoot. She pushed the knife into her chest and the world ended for Holly 13.

"Doyle? Doyle? Is that you?" A drugged voice came from the darkness.

Logan walked farther into the room. A dark-haired young woman was getting up from a bed. Her eyes were sleepy.

"It's me—Jessica." Her fingers carefully felt her new face.

A runner, thought Logan. *Her hand is changing color. But why does she think I'm Doyle? And did she get the*

"Key. Do you have the key?" he asked.

"Doyle … You don't look like my brother now. You don't even sound the same. They've changed us both."

So, she was Doyle's sister.

"Listen," said Logan. "Do you have the next key?"

She was completely awake now. He saw her take something silver out of her pocket. A key. Logan took it from her.

"Did Doc give you any information? Do you know what to do?"

"Yes, he told us to use a **tunnel** under Arcade. I know where it is."

"All right. Let's go." He followed her to an elevator. When they got out, he took her hand and they ran along the Maze **platform**. Logan pushed the key into a callbox on the platform. A Maze car sped out of the darkness and stopped. The door opened and they climbed in.

"Where to?" asked the car.

"Sanctuary," said Jessica.

The car sped through the Maze tunnels. When it stopped, Jessica didn't move.

"They can change the color of a man's eyes but they can't change the man inside. You aren't my brother," she said.

"He's dead," Logan told her.

Jessica's face became hard. "You killed him."

"No, but I saw him die. He gave me his key. He wanted me to have it."

Jessica started to cry quietly. Logan didn't know what to say. A Sandman doesn't feel sorry. He does what he has to do.

"Listen. Your brother's dead but we're alive. And if we want to stay alive, we can't stop moving."

"Please exit," said the car.

They got out and the car sped away. They looked around slowly. This wasn't Sanctuary. But *where* was it? Why were they here? It was a dark, ugly, dirty place. Trash lay everywhere. *What now?* Logan asked himself.

"Listen!" Jessica said.

They heard a small child's voice in the Maze tunnel, singing a children's song. *Sandman, Sandman, go away!*

tunnel /ˈtʌnl/ (n) a long hole under the ground or through a mountain for cars or trains to travel through
platform /ˈplætfɔrm/ (n) the place where people get on and off trains

Don't come back another day!

A small girl in a dirty dress walked slowly onto the platform. Her face was dirty and her hair was a mess. She had thin little legs and wore no shoes.

"Don't be afraid," she said. "I'm Mary-Mary 2."

Logan stepped out of the shadows. "What are you doing here?"

"Oh, he told me to meet you."

"Who did?" Logan asked.

The little girl's eyes became big and round. "He did! The old, old man!"

"What old man?" Jessica asked.

"You know! He's the oldest man in the world!" *Ballard!* The little girl took a key from her pocket. "He told me to give you this."

"Do we use it now?" Logan asked her.

The little girl didn't speak. She put her hands up and showed ten fingers. A yellow flower shone in her right hand.

"Ten o'clock," said Jessica.

Logan checked the time. "We have twelve minutes."

Jessica looked into the little girl's eyes. "Where do you live, Mary-Mary?"

"Here," answered Mary-Mary, smiling.

'Why aren't you in a Nursery?"

"I'm very smart!"

"But don't you get hungry?"

"You can catch things to eat. I'm really fast! But I never go upstairs. The bad people are there. They chase you!" *Cubs,* thought Logan. "Goodbye now. You're a nice old lady," Mary-Mary said to Jessica, and she walked away.

"She shouldn't be here," said Jessica. "Alone in a place like this. She should be in a Nursery with other children. A Nursery can protect you."

"Did it protect you? Were you happy?" asked Logan.

"Yes!" Jessica answered. "Of course!" She sat on the ground and rested her head on her knees. "No, I wasn't," she said after a minute. "I thought that everybody lived that way. I was never really happy there. Children should be with their parents. Brothers and sisters should be together." She looked up at Logan. "And you? When did you begin to think that Sleep was wrong?"

"I don't know, really. I heard the stories, of course."

"About Ballard? And about Sanctuary? Oh, I wanted to believe those stories when I was a little girl."

Suddenly there was a scream from the tunnel. Mary-Mary ran out, chased by a gang of Cubs. A wild-looking thirteen-year-old was at the front.

"Bad people! Bad people!" she shouted, and ran into Jessica's arms.

"What do we have here? Runners!" said the oldest Cub.

Five minutes, thought Logan. *We only have five minutes.*

"You're older than the others, aren't you?" he asked to the boy at the front. "You'll be twenty-one one day. What will you do then? You'll run. Just like us."

"I'm *not* a runner. Never will be!" The boy took something out of his pocket and put it into his mouth. *Muscle!* He ran toward Logan.

"Kill him! Get him!" the other Cubs shouted.

Four minutes.

Logan couldn't fight them all. He had to use the gun. He took it out and shot a *nitro*. It exploded into the group. Body parts flew everywhere.

"You're a Sandman!' shouted Jessica. There was hate in her eyes.

Two minutes.

Logan ran to a callbox and put his key in. A Maze car sped toward them, stopped, and opened its door.

"Get in!" Logan shouted to Jessica.

He pushed her into the car and it raced away into the night.

CHAPTER 4

An Ocean World

"Now, put your gun on the floor," he said.
Logan slowly and carefully did what Whale asked.

In the late nineties, before the Little War, the big problem was food. People had too many children. They lived too long. The great green earth could not fill their stomachs, and became tired and dry. Millions suffered and died. So people went into Space but the worlds there were cold, with strange, dangerous gases.

Then there were the oceans. Beautiful blue water, wild in places, bringing happiness and life. But below this … far below … there was another world, a dark ocean world. This was where people built their new city of **steel** and glass. They called this new world Molly, the queen of the oceans. She covered hundreds of kilometers. She took years to build. She gave work and homes to twenty thousand scientists and their families. She gave food and electricity to the world. Until 6:03 P.M. on March 6, 2033. Then a small movement in the earth **cracked** Molly's steel. Water came through, destroying more than a thousand buildings in minutes. Fourteen thousand men, women, and children were killed. This was the beginning of Molly's long war with the ocean.

The Maze car arrived at Molly and the seats unlocked.

"Exit, please."

Jessica looked up out of the car with wide eyes. She followed Logan onto Molly's platform without a word. The great Pacific pushed against the *plastiglass* all around them. The air smelled old. There were strange sounds like small explosions.

Why are we here? Under the ocean? thought Logan. As Jessica's surprise left her, he saw the hate return to her eyes.

"Yes, I've got a gun," he said. "And back in my room there's a black Sandman's coat. But now I'm a runner, like you."

"Sandmen don't run," she said.

"And Sandmen don't eat. And Sandmen don't get tired. Well, I'm tired and hungry … and hated."

She looked at him coldly. "You're a murderer! You've chased and killed people like my brother. They were good people. They only wanted to live."

"I didn't kill your brother," Logan said.

"Maybe not, but you wanted to. That's your job, isn't it?" He had no answer.

---

steel /stiːl/ (n) a strong, hard metal that is used to make cars, knives, and many other things
crack /kræk/ (v/n) to break along a thin line

"I hate you! I hate all of you!" she shouted. "You Sandmen live by pain. You never think about how wrong your job is! You love using your guns to burn people! You and your world are sick and I ..."

Her words cut him like knives. Logan hit her hard across the face.

She put up a shaking hand to stop the blood. Her flower was black.

"It's changed," said Logan. "You're on *black*."

Without thinking, he reached for his gun. Jessica's face showed that she was terrified. He stopped. He didn't know what to do. He was a runner but he was a Sandman, too. In that second Jessica ran off down the platform.

"Jessica!" he shouted after her.

The girl ran. Up stairs ... hundreds of metal stairs ... along glass tunnels with all kinds of ocean life swimming around them. At the end of one tunnel there was a large steel door. She threw herself at it and tried to open it.

The sound of a gun stopped her. A loud voice shouted.

"You! Stop! If you open that door, the ocean will take us both!"

She turned. Standing in front of her was ... what? A man? He was huge. His head touched the top of the tunnel. His face was like a moon, with two small eyes pushed into the fat. His mouth was large and blood red ... and his body ...

He stood there, holding his gun. This was Whale.

"Look behind you!" Jessica pointed down the tunnel.

Logan was running toward them.

When Whale saw Logan's gun, his face went red with anger.

"What's this? I thought that two runners were coming. Runners don't chase runners."

"He's a Sandman!" shouted Jessica.

Whale stopped to think. There was another small explosion. Another part of Molly was falling into the ocean.

"I'm a runner," said Logan. "I've tried to tell her but she doesn't believe me."

"So why should I?" Whale asked.

He lifted his hand and opened his thick fingers. Logan could see the black of his flower. Whale pointed his gun at Logan.

"Now, put your gun on the floor," he said.

Logan slowly and carefully did what Whale asked.

"OK, now let's take a little tour of Molly," Whale said. He took them back down the tunnel. "You drylanders don't know about Molly. She's a real fighter. She's like me. She doesn't die easily."

They moved slowly through glass tunnels and along moving walkways. They saw the cracks in the steel, with the water slowly coming in. How much time did Molly have? Whale took them farther and farther down. The water inside was getting deeper. It was halfway up their bodies now. They came to another heavy, steel door. Whale slowly pulled it open and pushed Logan into a small, dark room.

"Molly's sick down here. And fighting hard," he said. "This wall's going to break soon." He put his hand against it. "You've seen hard times, girl. But I've brought you help." He turned to Logan. "If you want to live, you'll help Molly fight. Keep your body against this wall. Give us all some more time. When it goes, you'll go with it."

"Wait! You're not leaving him here?" shouted Jessica.

"Molly needs him," Whale said.

"But you're as bad as he is! You're a killer!"

"A man kills to save himself."

Whale pushed past her and closed and locked the heavy door. Outside, he gave her a key.

"Use this at ten forty for your next car," he said. "Hurry now. You know where the platform is." Jessica looked at him, white-faced. "Molly's calling. I have work to do."

He turned, moved back along the tunnel, and disappeared.

Logan stood in the wet, dark space. His last hope was gone. He was a dead man. Now he knew how runners felt. He knew their fear. He moved slowly along the walls in the dark and tried to find the door. He couldn't find a way out. *Maybe this is my punishment*, he thought. *For all the pain I've brought.*

He could feel the Pacific pushing against the wall.

Suddenly the door opened. Jessica!

"Quick!" she said. "There isn't much time!"

They ran.

"Sanctuary," they said to the Maze car.

But it didn't take them to Sanctuary.

It took them to Hell.

3.1 Were you right?

Look back at your answers to Activity 2.4. Which sentence (a–f) below gives a reason for each of sentences 1–8? Draw lines between them.

This happens ...	because ...
1 Logan decides to find Sanctuary.	a She thinks that he is her brother.
2 Logan goes to a party with Lilith.	b Logan has a key to Sanctuary.
3 Logan tells Lilith the truth.	c Ballard started Sanctuary.
4 Doc agrees to help Logan.	d She has to give him a key.
5 Jessica goes with Logan.	e She gives him a drug.
6 Mary-Mary 2 meets Logan.	f Logan is a Sandman.
7 Logan is interested in Ballard.	g He wants to destroy it.
8 Whale tries to kill Logan.	h He has her key and needs her help.

3.2 What more did you learn?

Who is talking? Match two sentences to each picture. Then discuss what the speakers are talking about.

1 "I can make anything out of anything."

2 "It's changed. You're on *black*."

3 "You aren't my brother."

4 "You're going to get more than a new face!"

5 "But now I'm a runner, like you."

6 "I hate you! I hate all of you!"

3.3 Language in use

Read the sentences on the right. Then complete these first conditional sentences. Use the verbs that are given.

> If you **aren't** strong enough, **I'll be** in trouble.
>
> If you **open** that door, the ocean **will take** us both!

1 If Logan .... (find)

Sanctuary, he .... (destroy) it.

2 If a Sandman .... (catch) a runner, he ....

(kill) that person.

3 Logan and Jessica .... (not find) Sanctuary if they

.... (not use) the keys.

4 People .... (know) that Logan is a Sandman if they (see)

.... his gun.

5 If Logan and Jessica .... (not arrive) on time, they

.... (miss) the next Maze car.

3.4 What happens next?

Read these lines from the next two chapters and discuss the questions. What do you think?

Chapter 5 Hell

"Put your arms around her! Look into her eyes! Haven't you ever been in love? Do I have to tell you everything?"

1 Who or what is the speaker? ....

2 What is happening? ....

....

Chapter 6 Crazy Horse Mountain

They traveled farther and farther into the darkness. They finally came to a wider part of the tunnel, and there in front of them was a huge computer.

1 What is this computer? ....

2 Why is it important? ....

....

CHAPTER **5**

Hell

When Logan held Jessica close, he began to feel … what?
Was this the beginning of love?

H ell. The perfect name for this world. Thousands of kilometers of ice and
snow. The coldest place on Earth. Criminals were sent here. There was no
need for guards. No one ever walked out of Hell.

When the Maze car arrived at the platform, an alarm sounded. The car
immediately filled with gas. Jessica and Logan were drugged into a deep sleep.

Logan woke up first and looked slowly around him. Everything was white
… and so cold … What was this place? Not Sanctuary! The icy wind cut into
him. The Maze platform was gone. They must find a warm place … He woke
Jessica up and put his arms around her The wind was growing stronger—an ice
storm. They started moving …

After hours of trying to make their way through the storm, Jessica fell.
Logan shouted at her but her eyes were closed. She didn't move. *She should open
her eyes. If she doesn't open her eyes, she'll die. But maybe … just for a minute …
I'll close my eyes … Yes … rest … just for a minute …* Logan closed his eyes, too,
and slept.

When he woke up, they were out of the storm, in a huge ice palace. It was
beautiful. All around them were beautiful shapes of animals and birds cut from
ice. It was warmer in here. Some kind of fish oil was burning.

Jessica opened her eyes. She sat up in surprise as she looked around.

"Wonderful, isn't it?" said a voice.

Something was standing in front of them. It had long metal legs and a
strangely-shaped metal body. One of its hands was a metal cutting tool. Half of
its head was a man's and the other half was made of metal.

"A talking machine!" shouted Jessica.

"No, my dear. You're wrong! Not a machine! Not a man either! I am the best
of both! Perfect science! I am Box! I have the heart of a man, and the skill of the
greatest of machines! No man can produce the things that you see here. Don't
you agree?"

So this was Box. Logan knew the stories about him. A crazy half-man, half-
machine. He never slept. He was never cold or hungry. He lived alone in this
world of ice and storms. He had no need of others.

"Can you help us?" asked Logan. "We need food."

"Ah! You people! Is that *all* you think about? Your stomachs?"

"Yes. We're people and we're hungry!" said Logan.

"I don't need food," said Box. "*Art* is my food! Art is the only thing I need!"
Jessica looked around the shining world again.

"It is beautiful," she said.

"Wait until the storm winds come!" said Box, excitedly. "Then my palace
is filled with beautiful music! My art comes to life! You should see it! But men
don't understand this. They chase me. They only want my metal. They want
my legs for knives, forks, and spoons. What use are forks and spoons here? No
man can exist here! I've watched them die, so many of them. But now, here are
two fresh ones! Very nice ones, too! I will make *you* into Art!"

"If we do this for you, will you give us food?" asked Logan.

"I have no food," said Box.

"Then why should we do it?" asked Logan.

"Because my world will exist for thousands and thousands of years. It will still be here when your world has disappeared. And now *you* will be part of it. Two beautiful lovers, formed in ice, who will never die!"

"We only need two things," said Logan. "Food and a way out of here. You have no food and there is no way out of here. So, no."

"Ah, but there *is* a way out," said Box.

"Then why are you still here?" asked Logan.

"Leave my world?" asked Box. "This beautiful place? The silence? For what? Your wars? Your dirty, crowded cities? Your sickness?"

Box closed his eyes.

"There is a great mind of steel that is the government of the Maze. And I ... I am its brother. I know its ways. I can leave Hell."

"Are you talking about the Thinker?" asked Logan in surprise.

"Yes ... high up above the black mountain—Tashunca-uitco."

Crazy Horse Mountain*! So *that* was where The Thinker was.

"So, I will tell you how to leave this place. And you will help me make my Art. Do we agree?"

Logan looked at Jessica and then spoke.

"OK, we'll do what you want."

Box drew them a map and then began to give them orders.

"Stand over there together," he said.

Jessica and Logan moved to the middle of the room. Box stood in front of a large piece of ice and began to sharpen his cutting hand.

"Now, take your clothes off!"

"No!" shouted Jessica.

"You are lovers! You must be together—in love!" he shouted. "A prince and his princess!"

"Do what he says. Don't worry," Logan said to Jessica.

They slowly took their clothes off.

"Put your arms around her! Look into her eyes! Haven't you ever been in love? Do I have to tell you everything?" shouted Box.

When Logan held Jessica close, he began to feel ... what? Was this the beginning of love? Her sweetness ... her warmth. He felt a great sadness. She looked into his eyes. Was she feeling the same? Suddenly all the pain, the fear,

---

* Crazy Horse Mountain: a famous mountain in South Dakota. In the rock you can see a famous American Indian. American Indians were the first people who lived in the U.S.

disappeared. The Maze, the Thinker, Sanctuary … all forgotten. The only important thing was the two of them … here … now.

"Finished! Look! You're beautiful!" Box shouted happily.

Logan sadly took his arms from Jessica and they turned to look at themselves. Yes, they were beautiful. But there was no time to think about love or art. They had to get out of there.

Logan started to put on his boots. But then something hit him on the back of his head and everything went black.

When he woke up, Box was speaking. "… and death is also art. You will die beautifully my dear … slowly …"

Logan felt a sharp pain in his head as he turned toward the voice. Then he saw Jessica. She was swimming, terrified, in a clear pool of water with very high sides. There was no way that she could climb out. Box was moving a small oil-burning stove away from the pool.

"It's surprising how slowly water freezes, even here," said Box. "But don't worry, my dear! When the water freezes, you won't feel much pain. You'll slowly go to sleep. Woman in ice! Beautiful in death, as you are in life."

He didn't see Logan beginning to move. Logan reached into his shirt, pulled out a pack of Muscle, and took it. He felt the heat passing through his body. He jumped up and ran to the pool.

"Logan!" Jessica shouted.

He reached down into the pool, caught Jessica's hand, and pulled her up.

"Run!" he shouted.

"Aghhhh!" Box was running towards Logan. His cutting arm was sweeping from side to side, ready to cut Logan in two.

Logan got out of the way in time but Box couldn't stop his arm. It hit a huge ice plate that held up the roof. The arm cut through the plate and the roof began to fall. Logan ran. Box's arm was still caught in the plate, so he couldn't move. His ice world came crashing down on him. Logan heard Box's last cries as he ran.

Logan and Jessica tried to find the way out but the map was a lie. What now? They were in a huge white space. Everything looked the same. They kept trying, moving to the left, then to the right.

Ah! Suddenly they were out and standing on the Maze platform again! Logan quickly called for a car, found his gun, and checked it. The *nitro* was finished, but the *tangler, ripper, needler, vapor* and *homer* were still working.

"Where to now?" asked Jessica.

"To Crazy Horse Mountain," he said. "If we want to find Ballard—and Sanctuary—we have to go to the Thinker."

CHAPTER 6

Crazy Horse Mountain

Suddenly they heard a loud alarm. When they looked around,
they saw a huge robot, a Watchman, speeding toward them.

Crazy Horse Mountain was one man's dream. Korczak Ziolkowski used money from the rich, and thousands of workers, to make his dream. Year after year the men worked, cutting the mountain away. Fifty years passed. Finally, the brave Indian Crazy Horse sat on his beautiful, wild stone horse.

In Custer, South Dakota, the Maze car stopped and spoke.

"This is the entrance to government land. This car must stop here."

Logan and Jessica got out of the car. In the early morning light they began to walk overland to the mountain.

34

They walked for many kilometers before they came to a large sign.

U.S. GOVERNMENT
NO ENTRANCE
PUNISHMENT: DEATH

They continued. Logan didn't notice the dark shadows above them in the sky. Two huge metal bird **robots** flew above, guarding the government land. When they saw the two people walking far below, the order *Kill!* sounded in them.

They flew down toward Jessica and Logan.

"Be careful!" Jessica screamed at Logan.

Kill! One of the birds attacked Logan. He fell to the ground and his gun flew out of his hand. *Kill!* The bird was back. It attacked Logan again. Logan cried out in pain, but moved toward his gun. There! He had it! He pushed himself over onto his bloody back. The two huge birds blackened the sky above him. He shot a *ripper* at them. The two bodies exploded and thousands of pieces of metal rained down onto the ground.

When Logan opened his eyes again, Jessica was looking down at him. They were by a river. He could hear the water running over the rocks.

"You're going to be all right. Rest now. You need rest," Jessica was saying.

Logan was badly hurt. He tried to sit up but couldn't.

"Jess …" He tried to speak. "… have to keep moving … Ballard …"

"Sshh … don't worry. Sleep now." He listened to her soft, sweet voice and the sound of the river. "Sleep now …"

And he slept.

Hours later, they were moving again. Crazy Horse Mountain filled the sky above them. They found an old path and followed it to the entrance to a dark tunnel. The tunnel went down into the mountain.

"Are you all right?" asked Jessica.

"I can do it," answered Logan.

They traveled farther and farther into the darkness. They finally came to a wider part of the tunnel, and there in front of them was a huge computer. *The Thinker!* Different colored lights shone as it did its work. This machine, this huge electronic mind, sent information all around the world. It organized. It brought calm. It was the final result of years of scientific work at colleges in the 1960s.

They stood in silence, looking at it. Jessica was the first to speak.

"I don't believe this!" she said. "I can't believe that we've really found it!"

"I know," answered Logan. "But we have to continue."

---

robot /'roʊbɑt, -bʌt/ (n) a machine that can move like a person. It can also do work that people do.

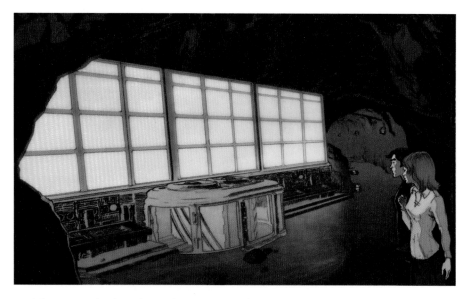

They went farther along the tunnel and came to a sign.

CATHEDRAL—JCV 498833
Los Angeles, California

They continued along the tunnel. Suddenly they heard a loud alarm and looked around. They saw a huge robot, a Watchman, speeding toward them.

Logan took Jessica's hand and they ran. The alarm got louder. They came to another sign and suddenly the Watchman stopped. It seemed to wait.

MOLLY—FJK 1704
Pacific Ocean

The Watchman didn't move. Why wasn't it moving?

"Of course! Molly!" said Logan. "This is a dead area. For the Watchman it doesn't exist. Molly and Cathedral are both dead, unvisited areas on the Sanctuary Line. The next dead area must be our next stop. Let's go!"

They ran. The Watchman immediately started racing along a different tunnel. It came out just behind them. And then it stopped again.

WASHINGTON D.C.—LLI 5644
District of Columbia

"Washington D.C.! Of course! Ballard must be there!" said Logan.

"But that thing won't let us out!" said Jessica.

"There must be another way," said Logan.

He saw a small opening. He could see small stone stairs inside, going up. "Over there," he said.

He took off one of his shoes and threw it down the tunnel. A light came on in the robot and it raced after the shoe. The sound of its alarm filled the tunnel.

"Run!" shouted Logan.

He and Jessica ran towards the small opening. They just got inside before the robot crashed to a stop outside.

"Can it get us?" Jessica asked. She was terrified.

"Not here. The stairs are dead, too."

"Where are we going?"

"Where the stairs take us. Up."

They climbed higher and higher. The space was tight and it got darker. Logan was tired and still in pain.

Suddenly he stopped. Someone was coming down the stairs! Logan hid close to the wall and looked up. As the person came closer, Logan could see a man. It wasn't Ballard. It was Francis! Logan took out his gun.

"OK, Jessica," he said quietly. "You hate killing. But this man is a Sandman and we're runners. Do you want us to kill him or him to kill us?"

Jessica didn't answer. Where was she? Then he heard her.

"Over here," she called.

She took him up through a narrower tunnel. It was completely black. They had to feel their way. It was difficult to move in the small space. There was almost no air. As they went higher, the walls became wet. They were near water. They continued climbing. They heard small animals moving in the dark.

After some time, they came to an open area. By the light on his gun, Logan saw a small pool of water with fish swimming in it. He reached into the pool and brought out a small fish.

"Oh God!" Jessica shouted. "Where are its eyes?!"

Logan caught three more. In the complete darkness, none of them had eyes.

Something ran across Jessica's foot and she screamed. Suddenly they heard noises all around them. Logan shone the light around. More animals were running along the ground and up the walls.

"I can't continue! We're going to die!" cried Jessica.

Logan pushed Jessica out of the space and back into the small tunnels. They continued, up and up. There were cuts on their bodies from pushing through the small spaces. They came to a wider space with another pool of water. Jessica fell against the wall. She had to rest.

Logan put his hand in again to catch a fish.

"Eyes! This one has eyes!" Logan shouted. "Let's go! Into the water!"

They jumped into the water and began to swim up the stream. Finally, they could see light at the top of the tunnel. It filled the tunnel as they got to the opening. And then they were out! In the bright sunlight and fresh clean air!

4.1 Were you right?

Look back at your answers to Activity 3.4. Then put the right words in the sentences below.

Watchmen	Box	art	Hell
the Thinker	dead areas		metal

1   .... is half-man and half-machine.

2   In Logan's world, criminals are sent to ....

3   Men chase Box because they want his ....

4   The most important thing to Box is ....

5   .... is the huge computer that organizes the world.

6   .... are robots that guard the tunnels in Crazy Horse Mountain.

7   .... are stops on the Sanctuary line that don't exist for Watchmen.

4.2 What more did you learn?

1   Circle the best words to complete these sentences.

a   Nobody escapes from Hell because *there are guards / it is an ice world*.

b   Box can leave Hell because he *has a map / understands the Thinker's mind*.

c   Box *is lonely / loves his life* in Hell.

d   Logan starts to *feel love for / worry about* Jessica.

e   Logan fights Box because Box *attacks him / is trying to kill Jessica*.

f   Logan and Jessica find their way out of Hell *with / without* Box's help.

g   Francis *can help / is a danger to* Logan and Jessica.

2   Discuss why these are important to the story, and to Logan's world.

A

WASHINGTON D.C.
LLI 5644
DISTRICT OF COLUMBIA

B

4.3 Language in use

Look at the nouns in the sentences on the right. Then complete the sentences from the story, below, with the correct nouns. Adjectives and verbs are given to help you.

> In the complete **darkness**, none of them had eyes.
>
> It organized. It brought **calm**.

1 Was this the beginning of love? Her .... her

.... (sweet, warm)

2 He felt a great .... (sad)

3 Suddenly all the ...., the fear, disappeared. (painful)

4 "... is also art. You will die beautifully, my dear." (dead)

5 He felt the .... passing through his body. (hot)

6 You need ....," Jessica was saying. (rest)

7 He saw a small .... He could see small stone stairs inside, going up. (open)

4.4 What happens next?

Look at the titles, the words in *italics* below them, and the pictures in the next two chapters. What do you think is going to happen to Logan and Jessica? Make notes.

Notes

Chapter 7
Who do they meet?
What happens?

Chapter 8
Who do they meet?
What happens?

The Gypsies

He took the top off the ring and held it under Logan's nose.
Logan knew that smell—Hemodrone, a Gypsy death drug.

Gypsystick—hey!
Lift me and play!

Logan heard the Gypsy song as he and Jessica finally reached the top of Crazy Horse Mountain.

"Get down!" he shouted.

He waved his hand and Jessica hid in the tall grass. Logan felt the burn as a *gypsystick* raced past him. His gun was knocked from his hand and in seconds he was in the middle of a ring of fire. Gypsies stood around the fire, laughing.

"If he cries, let's cook him!" they shouted.

Logan didn't say a word. He knew about the Gypsies. The first one was an Apache Indian who went crazy after the Little War. Other crazy young men and women joined him and formed a new group, the Gypsies. The Gypsies lived away from the cities, high in the mountains. They made their own rules. They were beautiful, wild young people who lived only for fun. There was no fear of death in the Gypsy world. They didn't run from Sleep or Sandmen, because they died the Gypsy death. They killed themselves when their flower was still red.

One of the Gypsies got down off his *gypsystick* and walked toward Logan. He was tall, strong, and very handsome, with long hair. He was dressed completely in white. He was Rutago, King of the Gypsies. Logan stood tall and looked Rutago in the eye. The Gypsy walked through the ring of fire, took Logan's hand, and turned it over.

"So, it's the Sandman's Last Day," he said.

He smiled and looked around at the others. A beautiful girl with long hair, black as night, moved next to Rutago. She was Graygirl, Rutago's woman.

"We're going to give you a wild time, Mr. Sandman," she said. Her eyes burned into Logan.

There were fourteen Gypsies in the group: seven men and seven women. The youngest was fifteen and the oldest was seventeen. The women were dressed in beautiful colors; blues, purples, reds. Their hair was styled and their faces shone with make-up. They wore gold and silver on their necks and arms and they smelled of flowers. Graygirl was different. Her shining black hair fell straight down her back and she was dressed all in white. Her beautiful black eyes shone. The men were all in brown, with long hair and tall, strong bodies.

Two Gypsy girls came out of the tall grass, pulling Jessica behind them. "We have a runner girl!" they shouted.

Logan wanted to help her but he couldn't get past the fire. There were the *gypsysticks*, too. These weren't the playsticks that he rode as a small boy. These were fast and very dangerous. They could burn a man to death in seconds.

"Tie them to *gypsysticks*," Rutago said. "Take them on a ride."

Three of the men stepped into the circle of fire. They took Logan and tied him to Rutago's *gypsystick*. The Gypsy girls tied Jessica to Graygirl's stick. Then all the gypsies got onto their *gypsysticks* and started shouting.

"*Gypsysticks* go!"

The sticks raced up into the sky, with the noon sun burning down on them. They flew around and around in circles and then raced along. The world was flying past. After some time, they arrived in a small town. The gypsies untied Jessica and Logan's feet but not their hands. They then pushed them into a bar.

"Now we're going to have some fun," said Rutago.

He showed Logan a large gold ring on his finger. He took the top off the ring and held it under Logan's nose. Logan knew that smell—*Hemodrone*, a Gypsy death drug. Gypsies used it on their enemies. Death with Hemodrone wasn't fast. The drug took time to get into the blood. Death was slow and painful. It sometimes took days.

Logan closed his mouth tightly. Rutago smiled and turned to Jessica. The Gypsy girls held her while Rutago pushed her mouth open. Logan tried to attack Rutago but was knocked to the ground by one of the men. Rutago poured the drug into Jessica's mouth. She cried out and coughed.

"You'll have to be a good Sandman or the runnergirl will die," said Rutago. "You do the right thing. Then I'll give you the medicine to stop the drug."

Logan was terrified. He had to stop the drug. He couldn't take Jessica away from here like this. He had to stop the drug from working first.

"What do I have to do?" he asked Rutago.

Rutago smiled and looked around at all the Gypsy girls.

"You give my girls fun!" he said. "And runnergirl is going to give *me* fun!"

The Gypsies took Jessica and Logan upstairs. Logan could only think of Jessica. How much time did they have? Was she in pain? The Gypsy girls took his clothes off.

In the other room Rutago kissed Jessica but she was as cold as ice. Her eyes looked in front of her but she didn't see.

"What's wrong with you, girl?" Rutago shouted.

Jessica didn't laugh or cry. The drug was working in her. Rutago kissed her hard. He pushed her down on the bed. Nothing.

Logan heard Rutago's angry shouts in the next room. Suddenly Rutago was at the door.

"Bring him down!" he shouted angrily.

When they got downstairs, Rutago was walking around Jessica.

"She's no good!" he shouted.

"We did what you wanted!" shouted Logan. "Now give me the medicine!"

"No!" Rutago's face was red with anger. "She's not a lover girl! You have to give me some fun! You have to do something!"

"Cut her, Rutago!" shouted the other Gypsies. "Pull her teeth out!"

Rutago suddenly smiled.

"No," he said slowly. "*He's* going to do it." He looked at Logan. "You're going to cut her. Take some of her meat."

"No!" shouted Logan. But he looked at Jessica. Her face was like stone now. She was dying. This was the only way to save her. "OK," he said quietly.

The Gypsies threw Jessica up onto the bar and held her. Logan's hands were wet with fear. Rutago was holding his knife out for Logan, smiling. Logan took it and moved toward Jessica. *Quick. It has to be quick.* He couldn't look into Jessica's eyes. He took the knife and cut a piece out of her leg.

Rutago watched him and shook his head. "No good," he said. "I don't give medicine for a bad job."

Logan suddenly caught Graygirl and held her by the neck. The other Gypsies backed away.

"You give me the medicine or I'll break her neck!" he shouted.

Rutago didn't answer. Logan took hold of Graygirl's hair and pulled her head back hard.

"It's in the other ring!" Graygirl cried.

"Give it to her!" shouted Logan. "Now!"

Rutago couldn't refuse. He poured the medicine from his second ring into a glass of water and walked over to Jessica. He turned to look at Logan and Graygirl. Then he lifted Jessica's head and poured it into her mouth.

As Jessica began to wake from the drug, she felt the terrible pain in her leg.

"Move! Now!" Logan shouted to Jessica. "Get on a stick and go!" He held Graygirl while Jessica walked slowly to the door. The Gypsies stood and watched. Logan waited to give Jessica a good start. He then backed slowly out of the bar, holding Graygirl.

When he was all the way outside, he jumped onto a *gypsystick*. Up, up it flew; strong and fast. He was scared. At the same time, he felt the excitement of riding this wonderful thing. He raced through the sky like a bird.

The Gypsies followed. Six of them. Right behind him. He flew to the right, then down. They still followed. Suddenly Rutago was there, coming for him! Logan got ready to fight. But no! Rutago raced past, toward Jessica! He crashed into her side and Jessica's *gypsystick* went down. She was crashing! No! She was up flying again, but there was something wrong with her gypsystick. It wasn't flying straight. Rutago was getting ready to attack again.

Logan had to stop him. He had to kill him. He flew down … down … faster and faster … into Rutago's back. He hit Rutago and took his head straight off.

The crash threw Logan off his stick and he fell through the sky into the river below. As he went into the water, he saw Jessica's broken *gypsystick* falling …

CHAPTER 8

From the Nursery into War

When they got out of the station, there were soldiers everywhere.
Robot soldiers. They were in the middle of a war!

Jessica lay in the hot sun next to her crashed *gypsystick*. One side of her face was bloody from the crash and her eyes were closed. She didn't see the fourteen bright eyes that were looking down at her. She didn't hear the soft sounds of their voices.

"Ooh … pretty," said the little voices. Seven small children stood around her. "What's this? Is it a person? So big! Person tired," they said. They felt her hair, her soft face. Then they pulled her slowly toward the Nursery, their home.

They placed her in a small bed. The bed felt her pain and put *synthaskin* on her face and leg. The cuts disappeared in seconds and Jessica slept well. The children stayed with her for hours, watching.

DAKOTA STATE NURSERY
AREA K

Logan stood under the sign and looked through a space in the wall. He could see Jessica's crashed *gypsystick* in the Nursery playground. She must be in there but he had to be careful. Robotmoms guarded the Nurseries. They sounded the alarm if they saw runners. He walked along the wall until he found a tall tree. He climbed it and dropped down into the playground. He had to be careful not to touch the wall: electricity ran through it.

He crossed the playground. Lights shone from the windows on the first floor

of the building but the second floor was dark. He climbed up to the second floor and tried all the windows. He found an unlocked one, pushed it open, climbed in, and dropped to the floor. He was in a small room with boxes in it. He opened the door and looked out. No one was around and it was quiet. He walked toward a Playroom and opened the door. The toys weren't moving or talking. The children must be in bed. The next room, a Birthroom, was also quiet.

His life began in a Nursery like this—and now he was standing in this place at the end of his life. He didn't have time to feel sad. There was no time to feel anything. He had to find Jessica. He left the room and continued through the building.

Suddenly he heard a noise. He knew that noise. A Robotmom was coming. He ran into the next room and quietly closed the door.

It was dark inside.

"Come now, my love," a soft voice said. "Come, my baby."

"But—I can't!" Logan said. He tried to escape but the room held him tightly. "I can't stay here. I have to … have to find …"

"Don't cry, my child. Sleep now …" said the Loveroom softly.

Logan suddenly needed his mother badly. He was so tired, so tired.

"Mama loves you …"

"But … I have to … I …"

"Sleep."

"I … sleep …" Logan fell into a deep sleep.

In Bedroom L-16, during her hourly tour of the Nursery, Robotmom K-110 discovered a young women asleep in one of the beds. She calmly left the room and switched on the alarm.

The sound woke Jessica up. Doors and windows started shutting everywhere. A computerized voice shouted: *Runner! Protect! Defend! KILL!*

Jessica jumped up and ran outside the room.

"Jessica!" Logan was suddenly there. "Run!"

They raced out of a side door just before it crashed shut, and across the playground toward the main gate. It was closed. Logan broke the glass and pulled a big black switch. The gate slowly opened. A Robotguard came up behind them but Logan was too fast for it. He pulled Jessica behind him and they ran down a hill and into a forest.

Hours later, they were standing in the middle of a station in Rapid City, Dakota. Logan had his gun again, hidden inside his shirt. Jessica kept her right hand closed to hide her black flower. But Maze cars always knew the color of people's flowers.

"Keep right behind me," Logan said to Jessica.

They walked together through the crowds of people. Logan came to a callbox on another Maze platform. When no one was looking, he cut the alarm. Then he took Jessica's hand and took her toward the Maze car.

But Jessica started to fall in the crowd. She put her right hand up to protect herself. A woman saw her flower and screamed.

"Runner!"

People started running toward Jessica and Logan. Logan pushed a man out of their way and they jumped into the Maze car. They left the angry crowds of people behind as the car raced down into a dark tunnel. The car suddenly slowed down … then stopped. The doors opened.

"Where are we?" asked Jessica.

"Sandmen have stopped the train. Hurry!" shouted Logan.

When they got out of the station, there were soldiers everywhere. Robot soldiers. Some were riding robot horses. They were in the middle of a war! Some robots were wearing blue coats and some were wearing gray coats. It was the Civil War*! Union robots were fighting Confederate robots. The air was filled with smoke. Jessica and Logan couldn't hear because of the noise of the guns. Jessica started to scream but Logan put his hand over her mouth.

Then Logan and Jessica saw the tourists. They were watching the fight and shouting with excitement. The Union robots were shooting across the river, trying to destroy the town of Fredericksburg on the other side. They wanted to get the Confederates out of Fredericksburg. Some of the robots were pulling heavy guns onto boats. A loud computerized voice spoke to the crowds.

"Today you are watching brave young men. They are dying for their country, to save it. Watch this fight, as it happened 254 years ago! And remember, there were no runners at Fredericksburg!"

Logan and Jessica moved through the fighting. They didn't have to worry about the robot soldiers. The robots' computers were only prepared for the fight. They found two of them, unmoving, in a tent. Logan took the robots' coats from them and threw one at Jessica.

"Put this on," he said. "We have to get to Marye's Heights, on the other side of the river. There's a Maze tunnel there. I know it really well. I played there when I was a boy."

Then they took the robots' guns and climbed into one of the boats.

"Follow me, men!" the Union officer shouted when the boat got to the other side of the river. "Let's show them!"

---

* The Civil War: a war between the northern (Union) states and southern (Confederate) states of the United States from 1861 to 1865

On both sides of the river the excited crowds watched. They were shouting and waving their arms. But wait! Was that a black coat in the crowds? Francis! How did he find them?

"We have to lose him," said Logan. "We'll have to go through the middle of the fighting. He won't see us if we move with the Union men."

The Union soldiers started moving up the hill. But the Confederate officer and his soldiers were waiting for them at the top. The Union officer was taking his men to their death.

Silence. Then the guns started. The noise was terrifying. There were explosions and fires all around them.

"Don't stop now!" shouted a Union robot from his horse. The scream of metal flew through the air and he was cut in half.

Logan couldn't see anything through the smoke. He couldn't hear. He was suddenly pushed onto the ground.

"Jessica! Jessica!" He couldn't hear himself. Could *Jessica* hear him?

He continued moving up the hill, along the ground, until he came to a wall. He climbed over it and rested for a minute on the other side. He then took off his Union jacket and threw it away. He looked over the wall and finally saw Jessica below. She was trying to move but the soldiers were running away from the fighting now. They were pushing her back down the hill. There were too many of them, all pushing, farther and farther back down the hill, toward the crowds of tourists.

Toward Francis.

5.1 Were you right?

Look back at your answers to Activity 4.4. Then put these pictures in order
Write the numbers 1–6.

5.2 What more did you learn?

1 Match the sentences with words from the box.

the Gypsy death	a Loveroom	*Hemodrone*
a *gypsystick*	a Robotmom	*synthaskin*

a   This is a guard. ....

b   This kills you slowly and painfully. ....

c   This can burn you. ....

d   This can make you feel safe and happy. ....

e   This happens when the flower is still red. ....

f   This can stop you hurting. ....

2 Are these sentences right (✓) or wrong (✗)?

a   ☐ Jessica finds her way into the Nursery.

b   ☐ Logan helps her escape.

c   ☐ Jessica and Logan find themselves in the middle of a war.

5.3 Language in use

Read the sentences on the right. Then complete each sentence below with a noun from the box and *who* or *that*.

> They were beautiful, wild young **people who** lived only for fun.
>
> These weren't the **playsticks that** he rode as a small boy.

tangler	officer	runner	*homer*	Rutago	soldiers	Francis

1 Catch him! He's the .... tried to kill the guard!

2 .... is the Sandman .... is following Logan and Jessica.

3 A .... is the part of the gun .... finds people by their body heat.

4 The Union .... is the one .... wants to destroy Fredericksburg.

5 The Confederate .... are the ones .... are wearing gray jackets.

6 A .... is the part of the gun .... throws a net around you.

7 .... is the man .... tried to kill Jessica.

5.4 What happens next?

Chapter 9 is called "Logan's Past Lives" and Chapter 10 is called "The Little War." What do you think? Discuss these questions.

1 What was Logan's life like when he was a young child?

2 What do you think Logan's life was like between the ages of 13 and 18?

3 Before the world changed, why were young people angry with governments and older people?

Logan's Past Lives

" I said kiss my boot! Then you can go," the man said again.
Logan could feel the men's anger and violence.

Faces, thousands of faces. But none of them was Jessica's. Logan was pushed along by the crowds. Everyone around him was laughing and enjoying themselves. A small boy tried to sell him a toy Civil War gun but Logan wasn't interested.

Suddenly a black coat … Francis! Logan quickly stepped into a doorway to hide. It was the entrance to a Re-Live shop. He watched the black coat moving through the people, coming toward him.

Something touched his arm. He turned and saw a robot looking sadly at his palm.

"We've expected you," said the robot. "Come with me, please."

Logan had to get away from Francis, so he followed the robot. He was taken into a dark room. The robot pulled a life bed out from the wall.

"Just lie here," he said. "This is the newest style of bed. You can choose the year that you like. You can also change years really easily."

Logan got onto the bed and lay down. When the robot started to cover his eyes, Logan tried to stop him.

"Listen—I really don't need this. I …"

The robot calmly continued with his work. He knew that everyone was nervous on their Last Day. When he was finished, he pulled a switch. The life bed began to move smoothly back into the wall.

Logan was in complete darkness. Suddenly he was sixteen again—in Nevada. It was the second day of his Sandman program. To graduate, he had to travel across more than one hundred kilometers of wild land. He was given no food or water and he couldn't take a gun or a knife. He had to find a way to kill animals for his food. He took his water from the plants. It was Day 2 and he was still alive. The sun burned down on him. He moved slowly. His mouth was dry and his stomach was empty. This was his test. He must pass it. He must not stop.

Then he was seven and his flower was blue. He had to leave the Nursery and go out into the world. He was scared. He couldn't take Albert 6, his favorite talking toy, with him. The little toy ran after Logan. It was crying and shouting at him.

"Loge! Loge! I'll never forget you!"

But they caught the toy and put it away in a box. Logan screamed and screamed.

Then he was thirteen, riding his playstick in Venice above St. Mark's Square. The wind carried him along and he flew around and around in the blue Italian sky. He was a bird! He was free!

He was fifteen. His teacher stood in front of him. Logan was learning how to fight in the Omnite way.

"Again," said his teacher.

Logan got into the correct Omnite fighting position and moved around the man. He was nervous, but he must do well. He must never be afraid. He had to learn before he could be a Sandman. His teacher hit him. Logan came back with a single low kick. The teacher caught Logan's leg and threw him to the ground. He then kicked his head and stomach with two quick moves. Logan cried out in pain and was sick.

"Never use only one move. Omnite fighting uses two or three moves together," said the teacher. "You must learn this."

Logan slowly got up from the floor and started to move around his teacher again. Before he knew it, he was on the floor again. He picked himself up. Then he was down again ... and again ... and again ...

He was six and it was play time. His best friend, Rob, was running across the playground away from him.

"I'm a Sandman!" shouted Logan. "I'm going to shoot you! Here I come!"

"Ha! Ha! You'll never get me! I'm the fastest runner in the world!" Rob shouted, laughing.

"Ha! You're wrong! Here comes my *homer! BAM!*" shouted Logan. "*EEEEOOOWWW!*" Rob didn't fall. He was running. "Ha! Ha! Missed me!" he shouted.

"Did not!" shouted Logan.

"Did!"

"Did not! A *homer* never misses! You're dead! A *homer* never misses! A *homer* never misses! A *homer* never ..."

He was nine. He was on his way to meet his friend Jack. Some men stopped him.

"Kiss my boot," said the largest man.

The four men stood around him, waiting. Logan shook his head. The big man hit him hard on the side of his face.

"Do it!" he said.

Logan tried to back away but they pushed him down.

"I said kiss my boot! Then you can go," the man said again.

Logan could feel the men's anger and violence. He kissed the man's boot.

"Ah ... This one's no fun. He can't even defend himself. Let's get somebody who has some fight in him!"

They left him lying there and walked away. They were laughing.

I'm not going to cry, Logan told himself, as his eyes grew wet ...

Then he was one. His stomach was full. He was warm ... clean ... happy ...

I must wake up. Must find Jessica. Must get up. Logan moved in his dark metal space. The Re-Live wall made soft sounds as the electronic messages moved through it.

He was nineteen and a Sandman. He and some other Sandmen were on a weekend break in Alaska. They were in a nightclub. He felt proud in his black coat, with a beautiful girl by his side and the other Sandmen around him. Good music ... good times ... perfect.

He was fourteen and his hand was suddenly red. Now he had to be an adult. Yesterday he was free and everything was easy for him. But now he had to work. But that was OK. He knew what he wanted to do. Now he could be what he wanted to be.

He was twenty and chasing a runner. The girl was smart. She crossed the river to lose him. But now she was caught. There was a high wall, stopping her.

Logan walked toward her. She was trying to climb the wall but she couldn't. She fell to the ground. He took out his gun and shot her with a *homer.* Then he stood there … He felt sick and empty. Why did she fight against Sleep?

And then he was twenty-one. Suddenly twenty-one! His palm-flower was changing from red to black. He was with Lilith, hanging from a tall building. He was running after Doc … fighting Cubs in Cathedral … He was in Molly, with Whale's gun pointed at him … He was in Hell, hearing Jessica's screams … Box was laughing … He was on the steps in Crazy Horse Mountain. The Watchman was waiting and Francis was coming after them … He was watching Jessica's terrified eyes as Rutago poured *Hemodrome* into her mouth … He was listening to his mother's voice in the Loveroom … He was watching Jessica moving up the hill with the soldiers … And then Jessica was gone … Francis was outside … and the robot said, "Come with me …" and …

Awake!

The life bed moved slowly out of the wall and opened. Logan sat up and uncovered his eyes. He got off the bed quietly so the robot didn't hear him. Then he went to the front door and looked out. Francis wasn't outside. He moved out into the crowds again. A police *paravane* was parked near him. Logan showed the policeman his right palm.

"Can you help me?" he asked.

"I'm happy to help a man on his Last Day," answered the policeman.

"I don't have much time," said Logan. "A police *paravane* will be fast. Can I ride with you?"

"Of course," answered the policeman, smiling. "Where to?"

"Not far," said Logan. "I'm meeting someone on the other side of the fight— over there."

"Get in," said the policeman.

The *paravane* went up through the smoke and noise and moved silently through the sky.

"Great, isn't it?" said the policeman. "I come to Fredericksburg every year. I feel proud when I think of all those brave soldiers." There was sadness in his voice. "*They* had something to fight for. They had a future. And what do we have? Sleep. You now. And my time will come soon. Before, I thought that there was something after Sleep. But now … I don't know. I …"

"Down there," Logan said. "On the other side of those trees."

The *paravane* landed softly.

"Thanks," said Logan, as he got out.

"Happy to help," said the policeman.

When Logan got to the Fredericksburg Maze entrance, Jessica wasn't there.

He went down the steps into the Maze tunnel and looked for footprints. He saw large boot prints in the dirt, from the boots of a Sandman. Francis!

Logan went to the Maze callbox. He broke the computer screen to stop the alarm. But where was Jessica? Could she find her way here? Was she still alive?

He found a place under some trees to wait. He could see the entrance from here but no one could see him. He heard a noise! His gun came out, ready. Then Jessica ran out of the forest. She was terrified.

"They're chasing me!" she screamed at him.

"Sandmen?"

"No! Some guys! They saw my hand!"

"Into the Maze," shouted Logan, and they ran down the stairs.

"The fight … I lost you … I couldn't find my way …"

"Forget it," he said. "You're here now."

"Washington D.C." Logan said to the Maze car when it stopped. They got in and he put his arms around Jessica.

CHAPTER 10

The Little War

Terrified people were running in the streets. The roads out of the city were full of cars as people tried to escape.

"Danger," said the Maze car. "This car must stop."
Logan and Jessica got out and Logan sent the car back down the Maze tunnel.

"We'll have to walk from here," he said.

They could see why the car had to stop. The top of the tunnel was down and the tunnel was in a complete mess. It was almost impossible to get through. After some time they found a narrow walkway that was quite clear. They followed that until they found a way out. They came out onto on an empty station platform.

STANTON SQUARE

Logan and Jessica couldn't believe what they saw. This was Washington D.C.? It was completely wild. Strange plants grew everywhere. There were no people but they could hear the sounds of animals and birds. It was very hot.

Washington D.C. was the place where the Little War began. At that time, young people *were* angry. A new law stated the number of children that they could have. College students filled the streets. Their angry shouting often turned to violence. Cars and buildings were burned. The police were attacked when they tried to stop them.

The President went on television to speak to the young. The world's population was almost six billion and there wasn't enough food. The problems were getting worse every day. He asked young people to stay calm in this difficult time. But his speech didn't work. The President was the father of nine children. Why could other people only have two?

The fighting couldn't be stopped. Politicians were taken from their offices by the crowds and killed. Washington was burning. Terrified people were running in the streets. The roads out of the city were full of cars as people tried to escape. The police could do nothing. Soldiers were called to the city but they were young, too. They joined the young people and fought with them in the streets.

The violence swept through the United States. Government workers escaped to save their lives. Offices were left empty. In two weeks young people were the United States government. Washington D.C. was completely destroyed in the Little War and nobody ever lived there again.

Then discussions about the world's population problems began. Chaney Moon had an answer. He was only sixteen but he was a great speaker. He spoke in London, Paris, Berlin. Soon his name was known all over the world. People believed that he could solve the problems. In six months, he had millions of followers. Most of them were under fifteen years old. Five years later, the Moon Plan became law. At twenty-one, Chaney Moon became the first person to accept Sleep.

Young Americans accepted this new law. Over the next two years, all people over twenty-one were killed. The Thinker was programmed to organize people's lives. The time of government by computer began. The first full-time Sleepshop was opened in Chicago and there was soon one in every city. Programs for Sandmen began. By 2072 the population of the world was young. Old people could never make the decisions again.

6.1 Were you right?

Think back to your answers to Activity 5.4. Then check (✓) the information below that is correct.

1 ☐ Logan was always a happy child.

2 ☐ Logan wanted to be a Sandman when he was young.

3 ☐ Logan enjoyed his work as a Sandman at first.

4 ☐ In the past, young people were angry about new drug laws.

5 ☐ Young people were angry about the President's family.

6 ☐ Soldiers didn't want to stop the violence in Washington D.C.

7 ☐ Chaney Moon was popular because of his ideas and his speeches.

8 ☐ The Moon Plan made it illegal for people over 21 to vote.

6.2 What more did you learn?

1 Match ages from the box with the pictures.

| 1 | 6 | 7 | 9 | 13 | 14 | 15 | 16 | 19 | 20 | 21 |

2 Discuss the other ages in the box above. What does Logan remember about those times?

6.3 Language in use

**Read the sentences on the right.
Then use (present and past) passive
forms in the sentences below.**

> Logan **was pushed along** by the crowds.
>
> Cars and buildings **were burned**.

1   A robot showed Logan into the Re-Live shop.

    Logan .... into the Re-Live shop by a robot.

2   The robot pulled a life bed out from the wall.

    A life bed .... out from the wall.

3   Then the life bed took Logan back into his past.

    Then Logan .... back into his past.

4   Special teachers teach Sandmen Omnite fighting.

    Sandmen .... Omnite fighting by special teachers.

5   Young people attacked the police in Washington D.C.

    During the Little War, the police .... in Washington D.C.

6   The Thinker organizes people's lives.

    People's lives .... by the Thinker.

7   Sandmen kill runners.

    Runners .... by Sandmen.

6.4 What happens next?

**What are these people going to do, or what is going to happen to them,
in the final chapters? Make notes.**

Logan	
Jessica	
Francis	
Ballard	

CHAPTER 11

In the Face of the Enemy

"You're a runner, just like me."
"But I'm not," Logan answered. "I guess I never was."

Logan and Jessica found some stairs going from the platform up to the street. They had to be careful. Francis must be there, waiting for them. Francis's skill and intelligence made him an enemy to fear. Logan told Jessica to wait below and silently climbed the stairs. The only sounds were birds and animals. It was safe for now.

"Jessica!" he called softly.

He watched her as she came up the stairs. She looked tired but so beautiful. She was still young. Why should her life end now? It was unfair.

They tried to find their way through the trees and plants. It was difficult to move in the terrible heat. They came to a clear area, and above the trees they could see the top of the Capitol Building, the home of the old government.

"Ballard is probably there," said Logan.

Suddenly there was a terrible noise. It was coming from the trees. A huge wild cat jumped out at them. Logan shot the *needler*. It flew into the wild cat's back. The cat went crazy, turning around and around. Logan shot again, using *vapor* this time. A cloud of gas flew toward the animal and drove it away.

When they finally got to the Capitol Building, Jessica fell onto the steps. Her face and arms were cut and bloody. Logan helped her up and they went inside. Plants grew everywhere, the windows were broken, and they couldn't see the floors through the dirt. They sat against the wall, too tired to speak. Jessica put her head on Logan's shoulder. It felt so good to rest. She didn't want to think. But they couldn't stay there long. It wasn't safe. Every time they heard a strange noise they jumped.

"If Francis doesn't kill us, an animal will," said Jessica. "What are we going to do?"

"The only thing we can do," answered Logan. "I know Ballard's here, somewhere. We have to find him."

They left the building and moved through the shadows outside. The evening sky grew dark and it began to rain softly. The rain became harder and harder until it was a violent storm.

Jessica cried out, "Ballard can't be here! No one can live in this place!"

Logan suddenly stopped. "Listen! The cat! He's back!"

He took out his gun. He only had his *homer* and a *tangler* left. A *homer* wasn't any good for this, so he decided to try the *tangler*.

They started moving again, as quietly as they could. They could hear the animal following them through the high grass. And then, through the trees, Logan saw a light. It was shining from a broken window in another large building.

"Ballard must be there!" Logan said with excitement.

The rain stopped. They moved out of the trees and walked slowly toward the steps of the building. When they got to the steps, Logan shouted.

"Run!"

"I can't!' Jessica shouted, but Logan pulled her behind him. The cat ran out of the shadows. Suddenly it was in the air, coming for them. Logan shot the *tangler*. The net flew around the cat's body and it crashed down onto the steps.

It was moving around, trying to cut into the net with its teeth. The net went deeper and deeper into its neck. Its angry noises filled the air as it tried to get free. It tried to jump up and fell back—onto Logan's leg. He shouted in pain.

A man was standing in the doorway above them. He didn't move. He just stood there, watching. Then he came forward, out into the light, and Jessica saw him. He had gray hair and the lined face of an old man.

"Ballard!" she shouted.

He was very tall and dressed in dark blue. He didn't speak. He had a gun in his hand but he didn't shoot.

"Kill it!" shouted Jessica.

He didn't look at Jessica. He didn't reply. Logan's gun lay on the steps. He walked over to it and kicked it away. Suddenly the cat gave one last long cry and fell onto the steps, dead.

Logan slowly pulled his leg out from under the animal. Ballard didn't help him. He just stood there, with his gun pointed at Logan.

"What are you doing?" cried Jessica. "That animal almost killed him!"

Logan slowly got up and Ballard's gun followed him.

"You can't shoot him! He's a runner!" shouted Jessica. "He saved my life!"

"He's also Logan 3, a Sandman," answered Ballard calmly.

His finger started to move. Jessica jumped at him and started hitting him. Ballard threw her from him but Logan was already escaping. He ran into the building and tried to find a hiding place. Ballard shot at him but missed.

Logan had to do something.

He felt in his pockets and found one last pack of Muscle. His body was very weak now. This was dangerous but he had to try. He felt the fire as the drug filled his body. He began shaking violently. He was huge—he filled the room. He moved easily toward Ballard. Nothing could stop him now. He calmly took Ballard's gun and pushed him outside.

"Oh, Logan!" Jessica cried when they came out. Logan could feel the drug leaving him now but he looked strong. His eyes were on Ballard, "Tell him," said Jessica. "Tell him he's wrong. You're a runner, just like me."

"But I'm not," Logan answered. "I guess I never was … Ballard's right."

The color left Jessica's face.

"I'm going to kill you," said Logan. "I have to kill both of you."

Logan looked at the red flower in Ballard's right hand. "I don't understand. You've lived two lifetimes and the flower is still red. How have you done that?"

"OK, I'll tell you," Ballard answered with a small smile. "It can't make any difference now. Something went wrong in the Nursery when I was born. There was a problem with the flower that I was given. I didn't realize until I was twenty-one. It didn't change to black. I lived while others around me died. I …"

Logan stopped him. "That's all I needed to hear," he said. "I've always wanted to know." Then he turned and shouted, "Francis!"

Ballard turned to Jessica. "He's a Sandman. It's his life. He has to do this. But he'll never find the others, the runners in Sanctuary."

"Then there really is a Sanctuary?" Jessica asked him. "A place where people can grow old? Have children? Live together?"

"Yes."

"Francis! Over here!" Logan shouted again but still there was no answer. "When you're dead," Logan said to Ballard, "it will be the end of Sanctuary."

He lifted his gun. One shot from the *homer* meant the end for both of them.

"Goodbye, Jessica," he said softly. "I have to do this."

But his hand was like stone; he couldn't move his finger. He tried to shoot but his muscles locked. He could only see Jessica's face, the pain and sadness in her eyes. He fell back against the wall. The gun hung from his hand. He was making strange sounds but no words came out.

"I *knew* he couldn't do it," Jessica said to Ballard. "It's OK now."

"You're wrong," said Ballard. "Half of him wants to run, to live. But half of him wants to destroy us—and Sanctuary. I can't tell you which half will win. You're not safe. You'll have to continue alone."

"But I love him!" Jessica was crying now. "You can't ask me to leave him!"

"You must continue alone." Ballard's voice was hard now. "Listen to me. The last stop is Cape Steinbeck." He checked the time. "You have twenty-eight minutes to get there. If you're late, they'll leave without you. You must go. You'll find a Maze car at the platform near Capitol Hill. Now go."

He turned away from Jessica and started to go to Logan. But Jessica hit him hard on the back of the head and knocked him to the ground.

CHAPTER 12

The Truth

He didn't answer her. He turned and walked
toward Francis. Toward his death.

Jessica helped Logan to the Maze platform and called the car. Logan's head hung down. His face was white. He didn't speak. They got into the car and Jessica held him close. The car sped through the dark tunnels.

"It's going to be all right," Jessica said softly to him. "You don't have to fight yourself now. And Ballard can't hurt you. No one can stop us. You're free."

Slowly he lifted his right hand. It was red … then black … only black. His twenty-four hours were finished. Suddenly the car alarm sounded. No—it was coming from something *in* the car. His gun!

"Gun …" said Logan slowly. "Wild Gun." That meant a gun in the hands of a runner. The police could hear this alarm. They had to get out of the car now. Logan pushed the stop light.

"What are you doing?" Jessica was terrified.

"Out!" shouted Logan. He opened the door and pushed her out.

His gun was screaming now. Terrified people ran from the noise.

Logan called another car but it was too late. A black coat was moving toward them. Logan tried to see clearly. He was still very weak. It was a large man. His mouth was tight and there was killing in his eyes. The Sandman shot his *homer*. Logan shot his. The two *homers* flew through the air, toward the heat of their bodies. They were moving closer ... closer ...

The explosion shook the platform and threw Jessica and Logan to the ground. There was nothing left of the Sandman.

Logan pulled himself up and took Jessica by the arm. They ran into the waiting Maze car.

"Omaha, Nebraska," he said to the car, and it sped away.

"We're finished, aren't we?" Jessica said.

Logan didn't answer her.

They began changing cars. On one platform, a woman shouted, "Runners!" People chased them. On the next platform, there were police. On the next, a *ripper* almost got them.

"Only fifteen minutes left!" Jessica cried. "They'll leave without us!"

They jumped into the next Maze car.

"Pittsburgh," Logan said.

The steel city. Nobody lived there now. It was one huge, noisy, dirty machine. Maybe they could escape.

The car door opened and they were there, in Pittsburgh. The air was filled with black smoke and the screams of steel production. The heat burned through them.

"Take off your shirt and put it over your mouth!" Logan shouted to Jessica as they made their way through the smoke toward the next Maze platform.

When Logan and Jessica finally came out of the Maze again, the sun was low in the Florida sky. The clouds were changing to red. Night was coming. Against this beautiful sky they saw the ugly, empty buildings of Cape Steinbeck—a gray and lifeless place.

"*This* is Sanctuary?" Jessica looked around sadly.

Logan looked around, too. He couldn't see anyone but he felt someone watching them. They began to walk toward the buildings.

A loud computerized voice spoke. "Stop. Give your names and numbers."

"Logan 3-1639."

"Jessica 6-2298."

"Give the word," said the voice.

"Sanctuary," said Logan.

"This area is dangerous. Do not move past the entrance. A guide will take you in," said the voice.

It was difficult for Logan to stand straight. He was so tired. His body ached. He started to fall.

"Do not move!" the voice said. "A guide will meet you!"

A man walked slowly out of one of the buildings. As he got nearer they could see his hard, angry face.

"It took you a long time to get here," he said. "Now, follow me and don't make any more trouble. This place is dangerous and you only have seven minutes."

They came to a huge building. Inside they saw flight equipment and many large airplanes. As they went farther inside they saw, at the very end, a huge, passenger space ship. Logan tried to understand. Cape Steinbeck was the United States Space center. It was a dead area, like Cathedral, Molly, Washington—all stations on the Sanctuary line. There were no Space flights these days, so the ships were out of use. But one passenger space ship seemed ready to go. Was it waiting for them? Was Sanctuary in Space? No one could live there. That was why Molly was built.

"Quickly!" said the guide.

They walked toward the waiting space ship.

Suddenly Logan felt something … Something was wrong. He looked behind him and saw him … dressed in black … He was coming toward them … without hurrying … Francis! It had to be him.

Then Jessica saw him, too, and started to cry. They were so close. Why now?

"Take her," Logan said, and pushed Jessica toward the guide. "I'll try to stop him."

The hard-faced guide said nothing. He reached out, took Jessica's hand, and pulled her forward. She fought to free herself.

"No, Logan! No!" she shouted.

He didn't answer her. He turned and walked toward Francis. Toward his death. The ground felt like sand. It was difficult to move. He fell down, got up again, continued. Francis was near now, his face hard, his eyes cold.

There was so much that Logan wanted to say to him. *This world, this way of life, is dying. The Thinker can't continue. People want to live. They know that this was a mistake. It is wrong to have a world only for the young. The greatest things on Earth were made by the old, the wise, the people who lived long lives before us.* But he was so tired ... so tired ...

Logan fell to the ground. His eyes closed. He tried to speak, but he couldn't.

"World ... dying ... We were wrong ... wrong ... Death doesn't solve problems ... I ..."

Someone was speaking. "Open your eyes! Open them!"

It was Francis. Logan looked up. Francis was standing over him. His gun wasn't in his hand now.

Suddenly Francis began to change ... his skin ... his face ... changing! Francis was ... *Ballard*!

"I couldn't tell you back in Washington," Ballard said. "I didn't know if you could leave your past behind. Now I do."

Logan realized that, of course, Ballard had to hide. He couldn't show people who he really was. A Sandman was the best idea. Nobody ever questioned a Sandman.

"I haven't been able to help many of you," he said. "My organization is too small, so I can only find a small number of runners."

"But—Doyle ... back in Cathedral?"

"I gave him a key," Ballard said. "I told him to try to get to Sanctuary. But you were too quick. Then the Cubs killed him."

"Then it was you, back at Crazy Horse Mountain, on the steps."

"Yes, I wanted to *stop* you then."

"But how ... how do you ..." Logan was so tired. There was so much to understand.

Ballard tried to explain. "I can only fight the Thinker in a small way. I organize a few parts of the Maze, the dark parts, but I'm learning more every day. You're right. This world is dying. The Thinker is dying. One day you and Jessica will be able to come back to a better world. I'm working for that. I'm doing what I can. But I have to be careful. I work mostly alone."

"And Sanctuary? Where is it?"

Ballard was helping Logan toward the space ship.

"Argos," he answered. "It's a disused space station near Mars. It's small—life isn't easy there—but people are free. And it's ours—yours, too, now. The stop for Argos is Darkside, on the Moon."

He helped Logan onto the space ship. Jessica was there, waiting for him.

Jessica ... Jessica, I love you!

Jessica reached for him and helped him into a flight seat. A computerized voice started the countdown.

"10–9–8 ..."

As the door was closing, Logan could see Ballard talking to the guide below. The space ship began to shake. Jessica's mouth was moving but Logan couldn't hear her above the noise. He felt the sudden movement of the huge ship and looked at Jessica again. She was smiling. He closed his eyes.

Ballard watched the orange fire below the ship as it lifted into the sky. It moved faster and faster as it left the Earth. He listened to the great noise as it went through the clouds ...

And then he turned and walked away, alone, into the night.

Talk about it

1 What do you think of the world that Logan lived in? What is good about it? What do you not like about it? Why? Make notes. Then work in small groups and discuss your ideas. Do you agree?

2 Work in the same small groups.

    a Look at these pictures. What problems of modern life do they show? Can they be solved, or will they always exist, do you think?

    b What do you think are the most important five problems of modern life and the world today? Agree on a list. Why are they the most important?

    c Compare your list with the list of another group of students. Explain the problems that you have chosen. Will they change their list?

Imagine that you are Jessica, at the beginning of the story. You think this way of life is wrong. You have decided to run. You don't know what will happen to you. Maybe you will die. You decide to write a letter and to leave it in your room. Write about your life, and about your hopes for the future.

To the person who finds this:

My name is Jessica 6 and I am a runner. Please read this.

Then I hope that you will understand.

You think that the world has too many problems. You want to live in a new world—a perfect world! Work in small groups.

1 What is your perfect world like? Look at the pictures and discuss the questions below. Then make notes to describe your world.

In your perfect world:

- where do you live?

- what can you see from your home?

- what kind of home do you live in?

- how do you travel around?

- what kind of work do you do?

- what do you do for fun?

- what is your daily life like?

- what kind of family do you have?

- what do you wear?

- is your life quiet, exciting, simple, fun, or useful?

Notes

2 Now discuss, and then write, six laws for your world.

In our world:

Nobody must work more than three days each week.

Supermarkets cannot sell food in plastic bags or boxes.

All 18-year-olds have to spend a year helping other people without pay.

3 Present your world and its laws to other groups. Decide which world you like best.

4 Imagine now that you work for a magazine, *Great Lives*. You have heard about some other people who have started a new life together in their perfect world. You want to write about one them in your magazine.

Write 5–8 questions to ask them.

GREAT LIVES

Questions

5 Work alone and interview a student from a different group about their new life in their perfect world. Make notes in your notebook.

6 **Now write about the person you interviewed, for *Great Lives* magazine.**

The Great Escape

It's a rainy Monday morning. The trains are late. You open the newspaper and the news is all bad. Have you ever thought about leaving this life behind? Here is someone who did!

.... built a new world with other people who felt the same way.